GIVING Thanks

How Thanksgiving Became a National Holiday

Words by DENISE KIERNAN • *Pictures by* JAMEY CHRISTOPH

PHILOMEL

PHILOMEL BOOKS
An imprint of Penguin Random House LLC, New York

First published in the United States of America by Philomel Books,
an imprint of Penguin Random House LLC, 2022

Text copyright © 2022 by Denise Kiernan
Illustrations copyright © 2022 by Jamey Christoph

Visit us online at penguinrandomhouse.com.

Library of Congress Cataloging-in-Publication Data is available.

Manufactured in Italy

ISBN 9780593404416

10 9 8 7 6 5 4 3 2 1

LEGO

Edited by Jill Santopolo
Design by Ellice M. Lee
Text set in Bell MT Pro

Art was created with traditional and digital media.

For Joe
—D. K.

In memory of Mom and our precious holiday get-togethers in the mountains
—J. C.

For as long as there have been humans on the earth, there has also been gratitude. People have said "thank you" to each other. They have felt lucky, and they have been grateful for all sorts of things.

Some people are grateful for food . . .

Some are grateful for the rain and the sun . . .

Others feel gratitude for their family and friends . . .

What are you grateful for?

No matter how they say it, it all means the same thing:

Merci
(French)

Meegwetch
(Algonqiun)

Meda w'ase
(Twi)

Gam-sa-ha-ni-da
(Korean)

They are thankful for what they have, big and small.

Sarah Josepha Hale lived in America in the 1800s. She loved writing stories. She loved helping others. She loved to cook. Most of all, Sarah thought it was important to show gratitude. Back then, communities chose special days to say "thank you" all at once. Those days were called thanksgivings.

Families and friends gathered together to sing their favorite songs and share their favorite foods. In Sarah's family and many other families, they ate turkey and cranberries and pumpkin pie. Sarah thought every family should make those foods for thanksgiving.

But when Sarah was growing up, thanksgiving wasn't always on the same day each year. Different places celebrated thanksgivings at different times for different reasons. Sometimes thanksgiving was in October. Some towns might have thanksgiving in November or December.

Some kinds of thanksgivings might even happen in May! There are always reasons to have gratitude, after all.

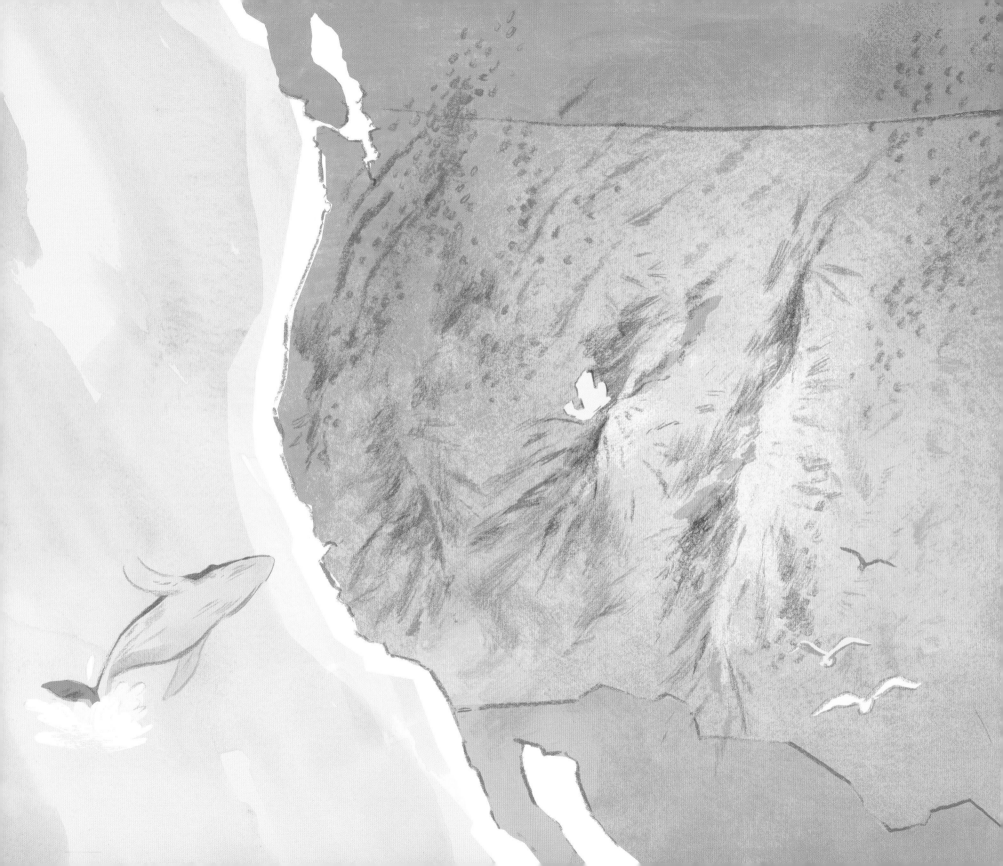

Sarah wanted thanksgiving
to be at the same time every
single year all across America.
She wanted everyone to share their
gratitude with the people they loved
on the same day. She thought it would
bring all sorts of people closer together if
they chose one day each year to share
what they were grateful for. But
what could she do?

Sarah could write. She wrote about thanksgiving in magazines. She wrote about thanksgiving in books.

GODEY'S

She wrote letters to people all over, telling them about how important thanksgiving was and that they should all celebrate it at the same time each year.

She wrote governors. She wrote Americans living in faraway lands. She even wrote the president of the United States!

Some people agreed with Sarah's idea. Others did not. But Sarah never gave up.

She wrote president after president, year after year. She wrote President Zachary Taylor, President Millard Fillmore, President Franklin Pierce, and President James Buchanan. Sarah believed someone would eventually say yes. So Sarah tried again. She wrote President Abraham Lincoln.

President Lincoln agreed with Sarah. He announced to all the people in America that they should celebrate thanksgiving on the same day in November—November 26, 1863.

But that year, the country was in the middle of the Civil War. The Union was fighting against the Confederacy. People were fighting with their neighbors—sometimes brothers were fighting against each other.

The country was split in two. Many people wanted their own separate country. Many people wanted to end slavery once and for all. It was a painful year, and in times like that, it can be hard to find gratitude.

Even during the war, people did find things to be grateful for, like having enough to eat, having somewhere to live, or being able to help others who needed it.

People all over celebrated thanksgiving however they could. Some celebrated in fields.

54th MASSACHUSETTS REGIMENT THANKSGIVING, 1863

Some celebrated on ships.

Some celebrated
in hospitals.

Some celebrated
at home.

But not everyone thought eating turkey was a good idea, like Sarah had suggested. President Lincoln's son Tad wanted to keep a turkey as a pet instead! So President Lincoln let him. And nowadays, the president of the United States continues this tradition and "pardons" a turkey at the White House each year and sets it free.

From 1863 forward, Thanksgiving has been celebrated in America at the end of every November.

Over the years, new things have been added to Thanksgiving weekend, like parades and football games. Some people choose this holiday as a time to help those in need. What is your favorite thing about Thanksgiving?

No matter what we do, where we are, or how
we celebrate, one thing always stays the same:
There is always a reason for gratitude, for
things great and small.

Thanksgiving Day can be every day.

Giving Thanks

How Thanksgiving Became a National Holiday

There are countless resources for anyone wishing
to look more deeply into America's history of giving thanks.

- For presidential proclamations and more, two wonderful places to start are the presidential collection at the University of Virginia's Miller Center (millercenter.org/the-presidency) and UC Santa Barbara's American Presidency Project (presidency.ucsb.edu).

- The Library of Congress and US National Archives host materials related to American history. The Library of Congress offers the papers of twenty-three presidents: loc.gov/rr/program/bib/presidents/papers.html. A great place to start at the Archives is with their Educator Resources: archives.gov/education.

- Some of the best information on Sarah Josepha Hale's life comes from her own writing. Forewords and biographical information, as well as editorial writings in the magazines she edited, provide insight into her personal and professional lives.

- For an in-depth look at all supporting resources, consult the endnotes of the companion adult title, *We Gather Together: A Nation Divided, a President in Turmoil, and a Historic Campaign to Embrace Gratitude and Grace.*